CW00666257

LADAKH

LADAKH
A WANDERER'S SPECTACLE

Nabarun Bhattacharya

NIYOGI
BOOKS

Published by
NIYOGI BOOKS
Block D, Building No. 77,
Okhla Industrial Area, Phase-I,
New Delhi-110 020, INDIA
Tel: 91-11-26816301, 26818960
Email: niyogibooks@gmail.com
Website: www.niyogibooksindia.com

Text & Images © Dipika Bhattacharya

Editor: Siddhartha Banerjee
Design: Shashi Bhushan Prasad

ISBN: 978-93-89136-46-3
Publication: 2020

Printed at: Niyogi Offset Pvt. Ltd., New Delhi, India
1st Edition: 2020
Price: ₹595

Death, be not proud, though some have called thee
Mighty and dreadful, for thou art not so;
For those whom thou think'st thou dost overthrow
Die not, poor Death, nor yet canst thou kill me.

–JOHN DONNE

PUBLISHER'S NOTE

I publish this book with a heavy heart. I never had the opportunity to meet Nabarun Bhattacharya of Guwahati, but was aware of his existence due to his communications over phone and e-mail with my wife and co-publisher Tultul Niyogi. She grew almost fond of him just by virtue of their talks and mails. I was also aware of our Editorial Director Nirmal Kanti Bhattacharjee's frequent visits to Guwahati, from where he would invariably return with fascinating tales of Nabarun's latest photographic trips and trekking expeditions, be it to Gurudongmar in Sikkim or Kinnaur in the Himachal Himalayas. Nabarun was his nephew. Unfortunately, as work on the book progressed and Nabarun remained enthusiastic about completing it soon, he met his sudden demise. The project would die a natural death with him, or at least so everybody thought. But I was not only saddened by the huge waste of human potential owing to this untimely death, I also felt dejected at the fact that the lovely photographs he had snapped and the telling chapter he had penned—all will go to waste. Hence, when in attendance at the cremation of Nabarun in Delhi (where he was brought for treatment), I took this exceptional decision to publish his incomplete work. The author had started preparing evocative, often even poetic captions for the photographs, but had time to do so only for sixteen out of seventy-two photographs. We have not ventured to add captions to the remaining ones, leaving them as they are.

Readers may accept it as our solemn tribute to a talented young man.

Bikash De Niyogi

Children of Dah

FOREWORD

This book is an unfinished project. The author, Nabarun Bhattacharya, who happened to be my beloved nephew, fell to a rare disease at the premature age of forty-seven. He was an avid photographer, a regular trekker in arduous terrains, an occasional columnist, and a voracious reader. He had won accolades in both national and international photography competitions, such that his friends put together a posthumous solo exhibition of his photographs in November 2019 at Guwahati, where he used to live.

A couple of years back, when Tultul Niyogi, co-publisher of Niyogi Books, impressed by Nabarun's wonderful photographs of Ladakh, asked him to write a text and put together a book with visuals, he was a little diffident to accept the offer. In an e-mail to me, he mentioned his dilemma in these words,

> I have no idea of what the Niyogis prefer. Scholarly anthropomorphological stuff was never my intention. Ladakh, Buddhism, Shiaaite Islam, Dogra rulers, Namgyal dynasty... all of these have been done to death infinitum.
>
> What was in my mind is something absolutely pedestrian. A topographical homage to the barren beauty of that place and how the landscape shapes the life of people making a living out there. BB inns, the Changtang nomads, the taxi ops, a whole spectrum of subalterns who are there for real but don't exist!! Google them, u dont find any. Google that place and u don't even find a proper route map on how u traverse the terrain to reach Tso Moriri from Pangong Tso.

This is what i intended to cover thru a 1st person account in an intimate involvement with the people, places, terrain, which i believe hasn't been done yet.

I could appreciate his position. Having studied in Rama Krishna institutes till his graduation, he had developed empathy with the ordinary people, their simple joys and sorrows, their habitat and lifestyle. So, he wanted his photographs not only to showcase the panorama and natural landscape but also to document the drama in the life of the common people of Ladakh. I asked him to send us a concept note, which he did. On the basis of this note, Mrs Niyogi signed a book contract with him. He accepted our offer enthusiastically completed the first chapter and sent it for our feedback, promising to complete the remaining chapters within 2019. But alas! Destiny had other plans. He passed away in May, 2019. These are the occasions when one feels guilty of living too long.

* * *

The land so barren, mountains so high, that only the worst of our enemies or the best of our friends would want to visit us—so goes an old Ladakhi aphorism. I once had the good fortune of visiting Ladakh, travelling its length and breadth for a fortnight. Indeed, spectacularly jagged arid mountains enfold this magical Buddhist ex-kingdom. Picture-perfect *gompa*s (Buddhist monasteries) dramatically crown rocky outcrops amid whitewashed stupas and mani walls. Colourful prayer flags fluttering in the mountain breeze share their spiritual messages. Prayer wheels spinning clockwise release more merit-making mantras into the atmosphere. *Gompa* interiors are colourfully awash with murals and statuary of countless bodhisattvas. Moreover, in Ladakh, it is easy to fall in love with the mountains. They are not only majestic, every mountain is of a different colour, and the sky looks so blue and close.

These are the things I noticed during my maiden visit to Ladakh. But Ladakh has many faces, and Nabarun had the perceptive pair of eyes to see those other faces too, as the photographs in this slim volume will show you. He visited Ladakh a number of times, sometimes with his photography group friends, sometimes alone. He once wrote to me in a rather longish mail,

> I am getting to know some of the most talented and kind people I have ever met: my experience with Ladakhis thus far lends credence to the stereotype that they are always smiling and laughing… However, it seems to me that Ladakh occupies an almost mythical status among most people who know of it, foreign and domestic alike. It is not-quite-India, as it shares very little in terms of culture, language and religion with the rest of the country. Some outsiders call it little Tibet, but it is not that either; Ladakhis themselves seem to shun the comparison… Setting aside for a moment my own growing love of this place, this mythic mentality is something I would like to challenge. As I see it, Ladakh is in trouble. Our outsiders' tendency to essentialize it as a pristine mountain paradise, devoid of real people with real people problems, is causing real harm.

I have cited the above mail to give the readers an idea of the author's involvement with his subject. Once, during a conversation with me about the traits of the Ladakhi people, he educated me by saying that the Ladakhi language has informal, respectful, and very-respectful ways of saying just about everything. Instead of just one word for every verb or noun, the language has two or three. How many visitors, tourists, or photographers go to such depths to understand the people of a place?

Nirmal Kanti Bhattacharjee

PREFACE

I am a nature and landscape photographer based at Guwahati in the North East of India; a leisure pursuit, I am sure, when seen in the context of the surroundings that I live in, is hardly surprising. What I find curious though is despite the immense natural reserves that we have in our part of the country, photographically speaking I have found my calling in a region two thousand five hundred miles away from what I call home. Ladakh!!

Well Ladakh has been kind of a happy hunting ground for me. To be fair, she usually is, even for landscape hunters who can barely manage to press the camera shutter. She stands out, always prim and proper, in all her barren splendour for everyone seeking an audience. In my case I guess it was just about getting bored of green tropics and seeking greener pastures in a barren moon land.

Ladakh falls in a rain shadow area, formed by the great wall of the Himalayas, the Karakoram and the Kunlun Ranges. Rain in Ladakh is akin to snowfall in Telengana. My first sojourn in Ladakh was washed away in seven days of equatorial downpour, and what a shower it was for my parched camera. The affair had begun.

To cut the flab, and at a considerable risk of self promotion, I would like to say that, over the years I have collected a large body of work on Ladakh. The collection of photographs mainly focus on a little bit of wildlife, a whole gamut of landscape, and people of almost the entire region. These are complimented with my field notes, research, and a skeletal text.

I would like to take this opportunity to brief you a little about how I visualise the proposed book. Tomes have been written on Ladakh already, and a whole spectrum of issues have been discussed. Tibetan Buddhism, Ladakhi culture (though the word Ladakhi is kind of a generalisation), Shiaiite Islam, the Namgyal dynasty, the Dogra rulers et al. My research says that, in the midst of all these scholarly historical and anthropomorphological debates, somewhere the average resident of Ladakh never found their voice. This prompts me to believe that there is still a lot of textual space left to bake a different kind of book, something much pedestrian, something that an average traveller can relate to. I see this book as a pictorial homage to the barren beauty of place, and how the landscape shapes the life of people making a living out there in that harsh environment. People who live there for real— the average cabbie in Leh who has to make enough money while the tourists land so that he can tend to his leaking roof before winter sets in, the illiterate Changpa matriarch who serves noodles in freezing Korzok and speaks Hebrew as easily as she does Japanese, the homestay owner in Hunder, a qualified engineer who volunteered as a guide for the Indian Army during the Kargil war and brought home the dead, the middle-aged Bengali lady from Kolkata who came in as a tourist, never to return back. This book intends to be their story in my frames.

Extracted from the Concept Note submitted by the author.

THE ORACLE

Hidden behind the flailing shopfronts, past the narrow gulley through a consenting orifice, through the dusty lanes with billowing juniper and dung plumes, beyond the staccato sheds of mud plaster and hollow bricks, a leap across the canal carved out of the Indus for sustenance and amusement, like a vagrant whisper a flat-roofed tenement betrays a quiet hum of activity.

Choglamsar is like a gnawing laceration on the face of Leh. On the Manali highway a few miles south of downtown Leh, abutting the model village of Saboo, Choglamsar is a bottleneck before the pit stop of Karu and Upshi. It is more Saharanpur than it is Leh. Amidst the detritus of truck-sized boulders left behind by the flash floods that thundered down from Saboo one night after a ten-minute cloud burst and tore apart everything that came in its way, a contiguous chain of wood and mud plaster buildings jostle for space with glass and chrome upstarts flanking the sides of the highway for about a mile. Not an inch has been spared, not an elbow room given. Here, the old world does not meet the new, they sneer, gnaw and confront each other, where each trying to outwit the other, appear to be caught in a time warp. Each of this macabre congregation of building blocks of varied shape, size, colour and architecture; houses and stores selling everything from motor spares to goat meat and alcohol to plastic mugs. When the

wares on display cannot be contained in the cubbyhole shops, they spill over the doorways and rest on the pavement, proudly flaunting the innards of the store. The pavement and the road is a heave and swell of frenzied shoppers, honking cars, bejeweled women, and dazed and contented jaywalkers. It is as if everyone is out for a doomsday bargain, everyday. The gut-wrenching come-ons of food stall owners and bleating goats straining to escape the butchers knife add to the revulsion that Choglamsar easily engenders without much of a fuss. In the land of high passes, it is here that for once, even the mountains bow to human intervention.

Five O'clock in the evening, two hours before sundown, the expectant assortment of men and women who had assembled under the square awning in the courtyard of the tenement has grown in numbers. The deep aquamarine entrance to the inner quarters frames a fierce looking Buddha and is firmly bolted from the inside. The bounded courtyard swept with white clay, which can hold at most twenty odd people, now looks crowded. People have spilled over from under the tarpaulin awning and have occupied every available space, making an effort not to stamp on each other's toes; while the luckier ones, mostly women and children, sit on their haunches in one of the projections of the irregularly shaped yard. In Ladakh, almost everybody has a nodding acquaintance with each other, or knows someone who is a mutual friend or a relation; civility therefore comes easy. While the men and women engage in small talk, the children attempt to run around or play Tag, only to bump into someone's back or topple over an extended foot, fall flat, get chided, sit still for few uneasy seconds and repeat the drill with the same diligence. It has been a long and uncomfortable wait, yet none of the men and women betray despondency; no one even looks at the entrance for it to open, let alone anyone even thinking of jumping queue, for there is no queue in the first place. A lot of

people here have come from far off places, even as far as Phyang and Taroo, a lot of them from Hemis, Stakna, Thiksey, Matho, Murtse and all the three Chuzot villages, quite a few from Leh; travelling most of it on foot, carrying apple-cheeked children over their shoulders. Every minute of delay would bear like a cross on their shoulders on their return leg. Even if they can afford it, finding a wheeled transport after dusk would not be easy. Yet, even after a wait of two hours, it's a cherubic gang that greets Ayu *Lhamo* as she walks into the courtyard from the narrow lane by the canal, apologizing profusely for the delay in a sing-song, whispery voice. Apparently, it was a stubborn spirit in her neighbour's house, which she had gone to exorcise, that was to blame for the delay. She looked tired and was already half panting, only to find herself with a courtyard full of seekers to attend to in the failing light, each with their unique afflictions, problems and propositions. In a fairly homogenous mix of people of mainly Ladakhi descent, Gurinder Singh, with his large frame, a proud paunch, black turban and flowing beard, almost stands out like Obelix in a barley field, the only two other incongruities being a nosey photographer who has heard about Ayu Lhamo and wants to call her bluff, and a hiker from Perth, curiously named Burma, who wants to get cured of insomnia. The Singhs run a motor spares shop in Choglamsar and have been staying there for two generations. Gurinder's younger brother is a truck driver who had a near fatal accident two years back. The accident, which almost took away his life, left him with a paralysed upper body and an unsound mind. When everyone had almost but given up on him, it was Ayu Lhamo who nursed him back to limited mobility and cured him of the post-traumatic stress. Ever since, Gurinder has never visited a doctor, and comes to Ayu Lhamo for every medical and existential problem that he faces. Although he found his fairy godmother in her, and despite her being a benign and calming influence on him, Gurinder was jittery and

And Then it Rained

worried that evening. His brother, who had been showing progressive signs of recovery for the past two years, seems to be going back to the deep dungeons of depression once again. He needs Ayu Lhamo desperately to turn things around once all over again. Gurinder's worry is whether he can find a decent audience with the seer in the large gathering that he finds himself today.

Not far away from where Gurinder sat, the last light of day was playing out her sundowner's symphony in the horizon beyond the steeples of the Stakna monastery, casting a biblical halo on the mystifying yet forlorn looking refuge of Lamas mounted on a hillock by the bend in the Indus as she leaves Leh on her north-bound journey. Like the evening prayers, it is a ritual that plays out at every twilight, and once every-day

Lording over Diskit

Horses at Kyagar

the consenting blues of the Ladakhi sky savours a game of peek-a-boo
with the flaring reds, the orange crimson, the nocturnal greys, ending
with a crescendo of inky cyan swooping on the unsuspecting city. The
last of the greenhorn Himalayan raven, which had lost its way, has flown
past the spires and Leh hesitantly switches on the tungsten yellows under
the shadow of the looming Stok Kangri range.

She was one of the earliest to arrive at high noon all the way from Phyang. The courtyard was empty, and the door to the yard was still shut. Lost in her thoughts she sat by the canal for a few hours, twitching her toe, watching children throw pebbles in the water. She watched as the urchins picked up pebble after pebble and hit them with a splash in the canal. She could clearly see them pick up one more and could

Slow Pangong

Indus Creed

anticipate the throw and assume the moment the pebble would make a splash, yet every time so happened it made her startle once again, and the strain of thoughts that she was lost in would get rippled by the splash, the same thoughts she would rather not be in. Sitting away from the crowd in a quaint corner just near the entrance to the compound, Dolma looked anxious, chin on the knees, her gaze fixed on the ground.

She does not even remember when a good soul opened the door to the yard for her, when she lifted her up from the banks of the canal and when she semi-perched herself near the entrance. As the other women chatted between themselves, and men guffawed and the children ran like chicken, the courtyard was empty for all Dolma could care. Cowering beneath the veil, she was not even fully inside the compound,

Lake Placid

her presence, a half-hesitant attempt of a hunted animal wishing to not be where she is. Other than the Australian hiker she was the only one who caught everyone's attention. Quite often men and women would throw furtive glances at her, and then, nodding knowingly, mumble something to each other only to drift away to something more fetching to talk about.

For a sorcerer, exorcist, seer, philosopher and healer all bundled into a single being, Ayu Lhamo is a diminutive and soft-spoken woman. She speaks Ladakhi with a generous infusion of Tibetan, which only a few in the crowd can fully make sense of. Once she is done with the apologies and a few greetings with a select few whom it seems she knows better than the most, Ayu Lhamo crosses over to the other end of the

courtyard, steps inside a brick-lined enclosure, picks up a beaten tin mug and pours water over her feet and sprinkles some on her face and hair. She crosses the courtyard again and pushes through the dragon-masked blue door, disappearing into the inner depths of her sanctum.

Meanwhile, a matronly lady who had the privilege of being personally greeted by the Lhamo as she entered, began the process of taking ownership of the crowd, herding them in a semi-regimental assembly line and dictating the dos and donts to anyone who seemed to her was in need of it or to whoever she felt like they were in need of a pre-admission briefing. Burma took her to be one of the acolytes of Ayu Lhamo. The lady did not look like she was a seeker herself, and had a nose-in-the-air attitude about her that suggested she was used to being talked to politely and expected deference from underlings. With the crowd and their aspirations under her command, she waited for a few more minutes and with a twitch of her brow ushered all in, even as she stepped in first across the low-hung blue door.

The room where Ayu Lhamo holds court looks like a cross between a living quarter and an altar. It is an elongated rectangular room that has received a fresh coat of sea green paint, and still smells of it. The room is so bare of wordly belongings, it gives the impression of being larger than it actually is. The floor is strewn with mats and rugs of different shapes, colours and sizes, often one overlapping the other. A forlorn cupboard with its glass door pasted with old newspapers stands in the western corner. The cupboard has a leg missing, which has been replaced by a brick covered in cellophane plastic to stop it from rocking and toppling over. There is a raised wooden platform resting against the wall facing the entrance, which has been covered with thick rugs and a few listless pillows are thrown around on it. The men and women who had been roughing it out in the courtyard, squat, kneel, stand or just squeeze in to fit into whatever space there is in the room and speak in whispers. They speak in hardly audible, muffled voices, occasionally resorting to whispers, making the atmosphere look more daunting. A fluorescent bulb hung on a wall struggles to light up the entire space as the last of the evening glow seeps through the lace-curtained windows, casting doubtful shadows across the room. Unsure of such surroundings and a little unnerved at the prospect of being in the divine company of ghosts, the Australian and the photographer fidgeted for a while, making sure not to cause any offence to the sombre setting, and then did the worst they possibly could do by sitting where Ayu Lhamo would perform her rituals. A collective gasp ran through the room followed by some frantic waving of hands. If getting shoo-ed away by an entire gathering was not insulting enough, an old man gave them an earful in Ladakhi, pointing to the exit. The crowd seemed to agree to what the old man just said, murmuring and indignantly looking at them. Someone else too took a cue from the old man and repeatedly pointed to the exit. Burma was about to turn away when the photographer pulled him by his shirt, asking him to wait out the barrage that in all likelihood was going to die down soon. With a silly half smile pasted across their faces, meekly they stood for a while like two chided toddlers, and then summoned courage to cat-paw their way to the raised platform and sat cross-legged on the edge, vacantly staring at the two doorways that lead out from the room into two dark enclosures, from one of which Ayu Lhamo's raspy breathing can be heard.

At the far end of the platform, next to where Burma and the photographer had first attempted to sit, rested a wooden table that is by far the most opulently decorated furniture in the room. The table is higher than the platform by a foot or so, has long curved legs and a glossy golden finish. The table is covered with a richly embroidered piece of cloth, and on top of it lie two large brass bowls filled with

Layers of Ladakh

rice and four brass goblets heaped with flour. Whosoever arranged the goblets actually did a fine job of it. Not only are they filled to the brim but the flour is stacked as an upturned pyramidical heap, creating an illusion of it being a vertically flipped ice cream cone standing daintily on the rim of the goblet. The rice bowls were at the centre of the table and the four goblets placed at the corners, guarding the bowls. This

was the altar of Ayu Lhamo. This is where she practices what she does. This is where she heals wounds and comforts sorrow, all under the gaze of huge framed portraits of the XIV Dalai Lama and Kushok Bakula Rinpoche, hung on the wall the table is butted against. A pair of butter lamps flicker under the giant portraits and a decorated rosary lies beside a mound of local incense that was already burning when the crowd was

Tanglang La

ushered in. The Australian heaved a sigh of relief that it was incense and not juniper leaves. Juniper gives him a headache and aggravates his insomnia.

It is ghoulish and unnerving, yet soothing and serene, as Ayu Lhamo begins her incantations, swaying back and forth and from side to side, holding her rosary in her right hand, held high above her shoulders and

chanting the verses in a sonorous, sing-song, raspy voice. Burma was a bit taken aback when Ayu Lhamo emerged from her inner quarters. This was not the delicate little woman he had seen greet people in the courtyard. Indeed, Ayu Lhamo definitely looked much larger and almost imposing in the gold-and-blue bejeweled gown that she had put on over her *kuntop*, the dress that all Ladakhi women wear. She had

Nubra

taken off the traditional *perak* hat and had covered her head with a glitzy looking crown made of a golden gift-wrap paper pasted on a cardboard cut-out tailored to fit her forehead. The entire contraption was tied at the back of her upper shoulders with cheap beaded tassels.

The Australian had picked up a conversation with the photographer in the courtyard and was at varied degrees of disagreement over oriental mysticism that sells well. Ayu Lhamo's preposterous crown with its jagged golden edges brought a bemused scowl to his face. Burma stole a glance at the photographer and exchanged a derisive smirk, and then blushed sheepishly at his Ladakhi guide who was watching him do that.

After fifteen minutes of chanting, Ayu Lhamo's voice had gathered a shrill edge to it. The lilting cadence of her initial incantations was gaining pitch with every sentence that she delivered. She was swaying more pronouncedly, shaking her head sideways every now and then and intermittently ringing a small bell with her left hand, keeping her right hand upright all the time. The burning incense had caused enough smoke in the room already when someone brought a fuming charcoal stove and placed it near the altar, within the reach of the Lhamo. Two large daggers with wooden butts were being heated in the angry embers of the stove, which was hissing and puffing and belching more smoke all over the room. While nobody even bothered so much as to even look at it, Burma almost jumped and made a dash for the exit at the sight of the sputtering charcoal, cooking daggers.

"This is now spirit enter Lhamo," whispered Burma's guide, "She now call them."

Ayu Lhamo had momentarily stopped chanting, although she already appeared to be in a stupor. Her eyes were bloodshot and she was sweating profusely. She fiddled with the rosary for a moment, pushed the daggers further down into the stove, looked absently at the crowd,

and resumed her sing-song mantras in a piercing yet sombre voice with feverish ringing of the bell,

The speckled moon,
Sinister, in anointed gloom
Nudges the reigning star
Past the craggy peaks,
The oblivion,
Dank, dark and deep.

Hark you from
The dungeons of the past!
Coyote fangs, sinister wail
White as black, blood as red
Dig deep the marrows, and
Ride your dreams...

No more willowy wisps
Not an ounce of
Sugary lisps,
The yellowed halo is what I am
The inky glow here,
Dreads a peep!

That voyeur tonight
Once you called a bluff,
In a hurry and in a huff
Was me...
Not you!
Not you!

Beyond the garb, under the veil
Beneath the shroud, your
Conceited wail,
You dreamt of you
Not me!
Not me!

Burma had no way of confirming the accuracy of his guide's translation of Tibetan chants. He however was sure that, if that was an invite, the spirits better behave! He did not know what was further in store for him to see, but he saw Ayu Lhamo's transition from a feeble old lady into a gathering storm and did not want to have any more of it, especially with those barbecued daggers nearby. "He come now. Spirit

Khardung La

come," whispered Burma's guide in his ears and waved angrily at the photographer not to switch on the camera flash, ever.

It is not easy being an oracle. It takes years and years of abnegation, dedication, and prolonged periods of hard labour and practice to master the art of healing. An art that does not give much in return, does not pay well either, but then renunciation is what an oracle is obliged to perfect before they are allowed to begin the long and arduous physical and mental journey of summoning spirits to heal fellow human beings. To begin with, a prospective oracle has to show promise in their early childhood. The promise has to be noted and approved by a high-ranking Lama. Ayu Lhamo showed this promise by getting into frequent fits when she was very young. During some of those fits she made some small prophecies in a half-delirious state, which came true and made her a minor celebrity. It is then that she was taken to a Lama in Thiksey Monastery, who instantly knew that here was a great oracle in the making. Upon his advice she was sent to another Lama who led a reclusive life high up in the mountains. It was under his tutelage Ayu Lhamo began the torturous journey of being a faith healer. She spent her entire youth in the mountains, mostly alone, studying Buddhist scriptures, the art of meditation, how to get into a trance, and how to distinguish between good and evil spirits and be a channel for various divine beings without being a slave to their command. When she was young, her fits were not out of her own volition; she used to just collapse and foam at the mouth and spell incoherent narratives. When she finally came down from the mountains one day, she could inflict a trance on herself at will and survive severe self-flagellation. It was apparent that she could prophesize, make divination, purify homesteads, yet she could not practice what she was taught. That needed sanction from the monastic order. Ayu Lhamo was lucky, and was destined to be what she is. Her tender steps at being

a Lhamo was approved by none other than the Dalai Lama himself. There was no looking back thereafter.

As Ayu Lhamo's elaborate invite to the spirits was nearing the end, every visitor had quietly started picking up a white *khata* each from a stool beside the altar, placing a tenner or a twenty-rupee bill in exchange. Burma's guide fetched two, one for his client and the other for the photographer and asked them to hold it in two folds. There is a set of protocol to be followed while handling and presenting the khata or the Tibetan scarf, and the guide could not afford another faux pas from his client. A khata comes in various colours and is offered on various occasions, each having its unique etiquette and decorum. When a khata is offered out of gratitude or respect towards monks or dignitaries, it is usually offered with folded hands with a bow of the head. Normally on such occasions, the khata offered to the monk or any spiritual being is received back by the giver with a blessing. Burma was greeted at his hotel with a khata around his neck. His guide now dreaded that it was absolutely possible for his client to do the same to Ayu Lhamo—welcome her in her own residence !

After forty minutes of heaving and swaying and rocking back and forth, Ayu Lhamo turned towards the crowd. Although rivulets of sweat were dripping down from her forehead, she was not breathing as heavily as before. She sat on bent knees, a hint of smile on her lips. She still had the crown and the robe on her, and was mumbling something under the breath, her eyes shut, her face a perfect frame of peace within. The spirit it seemed had calmed her; Burma hoped it was a benevolent one.

The smoke made everyone in the room wheeze and cough and had turned their eyes red. When Ayu Lhamo opened her eyes, her reds were gone. Without showing any discomfiture, she casually picked up one of the red-hot daggers and slashed her tongue with the rusty iron.

The dagger hissed in her mouth and a puff of smoke came out of it. Ayu Lhamo placed the dagger back into the oven, grimaced almost as a flehmen response, then took a deep breath and in her original whispery raspy voice said, "Let's begin."

Prodded by the matronly lady, weeping Dolma got to speak first, but even before she could gather herself together Ayu Lhamo raised her hand indicating her to stop. Between her sobs Dolma tried to mutter something; Ayu Lhamo did not hear a word of it. She picked up a tambourine-shaped drum instead, picked some rice grains from the bowl on the altar, put a pinch of the grains on the flat bed of the drum and flipped the rice from the drum high up in the air. The flying grains landed back with a patter on the drum. Ayu Lhamo counted the grains, then grouped them in batches of three with her finger, throwing the rest of it away she again flipped the grains up. This time fewer grains landed on the drum. She counted them again, poured it in her palm and gave it to Dolma asking her to chew them without making any sound. Dolma tried to do the job given to her as diligently as she could, but everytime an obstinate grain made a crackling sound in her mouth, Ayu Lhamo grimaced as if in pain. When all the grain was chewed and gulped down, Dolma came forward and with a bow of her head offered Ayu Lhamo the khata in two folds with folded hands, all the time sobbing uncontrollably. "You shall stay away from your husband till the next full moon," Ayu Lhamo commanded.

"You shall remain pure all the time, and shall not touch your husband or serve him any food if it is that time of the month for you. You shall not ask him to stop drinking. The more you insist the more he will turn to alcoholism."

Dolma had stopped sobbing and was absorbing every word the Lhamo spoke with a wide-mouthed awe, her head scarf clenched between her teeth revealing only half of her face.

"As about the scars that he gave you, you have been healed, and they shall disappear in a day or two. For the cigarette burns on your breasts, you husband shall pay dearly for that."

Dolma started howling now. Some of the women patted her head and asked her to calm down. Ayu Lhamo picked up the khata that Dolma had offered her, put it against her mouth and mumbled

something into it. Then she tied three knots in the khata and placed it on Dolma's hand. "Every act of birth is preceded by a transgression, a man lives but only for atonement!"

"As you go home today, buy a new shirt for him, and put this khata in the pocket. Insist upon him wearing this at least once every day for the next fifteen days. If he doesn't, then quietly put this shirt beside his

The Marauders from Mordor

pillow when he sleeps. Remember not to touch this shirt when you are impure. He will be cured."

Ayu Lhamo brought Dolma closer to her, held her head with both her palms and removed the headscarf from her face as Dolma flinched. Then she profusely spat all over her face and body, and with a wave of her hand dismissed her. When Dolma hurriedly shuffled out of the

room she did not feel it necessary to cover her face again. There was a deep gnawing gash on her left cheek.

With the small matter of sobbing Dolma sorted out, the matron in the group assumed she was entitled to the perquisite of speaking to the Lhamo before anyone else did. Even though she arrived much after a lot many people in the group, she thought she had already done

Turtuk Fairy

Snow White

her grace by allowing Dolma to be healed first. Naturally predisposed towards gentility, Ladakhi people normally do not fly into road rage at minor infringements like jumping of queue, and occasions such as this naturally do not behove bickering over petty existential issues. In any case, people who usually visit Ayu Lhamo resign themselves to long periods of waiting. Moreover, the matron looked like she was gifted with an ability of being able to thwart any attempts at threatening her preeminence everywhere. That she spoke fluent Tibetan made it more difficult for other people to speak over her in Ayu Lhamo's presence.

The calmness with which Ayu Lhamo handled Dolma in the meantime had reassured Burma to quite an extent. He was imagining all kinds of things and was particularly worried that the pair of red-hot metals would be used on the patients. His photographer friend too picked up some courage and started to tiptoe around the room clicking pictures without the flashbulb. The photographer did not look too happy with the output though. Each time he fired a burst of shots, they came out fuzzy, as Ayu Lhamo was not exactly posing for portraits. When he jacked up the ISO to compensate for the poor ambient light, the photos became grainy. As he fiddled with the camera's settings, thinking of a way to manage at least one decent shot, the matron started rattling away the symptoms of every ailment she had or suspected to have. Ayu Lhamo gave her a patient hearing and then took out a piece of cloth that was worn around her neck. The cloth was actually a piece of a khata that had seen better days. She pressed the khata on the platform with both her hands, and rubbed her palms over it a number of times to remove the crease. That done, she rolled it into a flattened straw-like shape, gripped one end of the cloth with her lips and pressed the other end mildly on the matron's back and started sucking the ailment out of the body. She tapped and placed the handheld end of the cloth on

Armageddon

different parts of the woman's body, just as any doctor would do with a stethoscope, and each time that she found a vulnerable spot, she drew in hard. Each breath she took, the piece of khata made a deep gurgling sound; the sound children make when they blow air through a straw into their half-finished glass of juice. Initially when she had started doing so, every time Ayu Lhamo tapped on the back of the woman,

the matron would cringe instinctively and wince as though someone had poked an open wound. By the time the Lhamo had sucked in ten to fifteen times from her back, the matron was in considerable pain and had started writhing and shivering. After one or two more such draws, the matron let out a ghastly wail, keeled over, doubled up and fell face first on the lap of the woman next to her. A minor bedlam ran through

the house for the next few minutes. People started making space for the matron to lie down, while some ran out to fetch water; some started to fan the woman with a piece of newspaper; the photographer forgot to shoot the sequence, and Burma almost fainted. The matron was finally laid supine properly, and for half an hour remained motionless, relieved of all her imperiousness. In the midst of all this, no one had noticed

that Ayu Lhamo had started chanting and swaying again in a tenor considerably lower than her introductory incantations. A hush once again blanketed the room. Ayu Lhamo prayed with her eyes closed for some time, then got up from her seat, rushed out of the room into the courtyard and holding her tummy, retching violently, she disgorged a large amount of black, gooey fluid in the concrete drain at the edge

of the courtyard. She waited there for sometime looking extremely exhausted, sprinkled some water once again on her face and head and came back into the room.

"Haven't seen a naughtier one for quite some time now," she said looking at the recumbent matron, "Made me vomit, didn't you? Now let me see what brings you back to Leh again."

The matron showed first signs of life only after Ayu Lhamo had treated a whole gaggle of her clients meanwhile. Some with grains of rice, some with suction, some with holy head massage, each following a fixed pattern. By the time the matron regained her consciousness, Ayu Lhamo had cured people of ailments ranging from back pain to loss of appetite, from amnesia to sleepwalking, from common flu to rabid

cough; almost the entire gamut of afflictions needing cardiothoracic to neuropsychiatric intervention was healed or cleansed with a tambourine, some rice, two daggers and a piece of ragged cloth. Ayu Lhamo had also asked Gurinder to leave, as she had already spoken to his father on her way back. His brother's treatment would need a special session which can only be performed on the auspicious sixteenth of the month,

and that she shall call him only after a visitation of a competent spirit. Gurinder, dejected, bowed twice and left the room quietly.

Before she regained her composure, the matron got up and sat straight leaning against the wall. The initial words she tried to say were beyond anyone to decipher. She looked awed and a little befuddled to see the crowded room almost empty. She clearly seemed

unable to figure out what was amiss. Ayu Lhamo waved her to come closer, patted her head with both her hands, arranged her disheveled hair and said "See darling, you have no pain. You have redeemed yourself. Your agony is a thing of past now." Ayu Lhamo pressed hard against the woman's back and chest, "Do you feel anything? You wouldn't."

Still in half stupor, the woman nodded in agreement and forced a
smile. She looked lost and seemed to have been robbed of her character.
The subtle cockiness, that smug disdainful confidence seemed to have
departed her, for now at least. She was smiling back at people in the
room. "Why don't you adopt a child, darling? That'll suit you fine.
Motherhood shall be great for you to reinvent yourself. You'll find the

world such a better place, you see! Still better, if you can adopt a few more. You don't have to take all of them home. I don't have to tell you about needy kids, do I? Feed them, give them clothes, send them to school. You shall find purpose to your life once again. Think about it."

The matron started weeping. She sat there with her head bowed for a few minutes and wept her heart out. "You may leave now," Ayu Lhamo motioned someone to escort the lady out to ensure that she crosses the canal safely.

The room was now almost empty. Other than Burma, his photographer friend and his guide, there were hardly two to three people left. Ayu Lhamo looked at the two. This was the moment Burma was dreading most. Even though he was considerably convinced that the daggers would not be used on him, the episode with the matron had left him a little disconcerted. He did not want the spirit or whatever Ayu Lhamo was holding within her to jump seat and claim residence in him. As Ayu Lhamo looked at them, he pushed his photographer friend to the front. The photographer had come to see the Lhamo out of pure curiosity and may be for a few good pictures, and although he was actually quite impressed seeing her providing psychological counseling to her clients, he still believed that Ayu Lhamo was nothing but a showboat. Thrust in the front, he fumbled for quite some time trying to cook up an ailment that came to his mind first, all the time Ayu Lhamo following his eyes with a piercing gaze. Despite his best intentions, something in him stopped him from doing so. He thought about his ailing mother, who was confined to bed for the past so many years with a debilitating arthritis. He had taken her all over the country, consulted the best doctors and gave her the best treatment available. Yet her symptoms kept on deteriorating, to the extent that she needed assistance to even turn over in her bed. The prognosis was bad, and he understood there was no chance of it getting any better; and now,

here he was, oscillating between an option of dismissing Ayu Lhamo altogether by faking his own ailment or seeking genuine help for his mother by being a believer once all over again. With Burma's guide acting as the interpreter, the photographer gave a sketchy picture of his mother, caring not to reveal too much about how serious a condition she was in. Ayu Lhamo heard him out and went into a brief meditation

closing her eyes. When she was back, she picked the dagger from the coal and blanched her tongue with it once again. Having tasted iron, she went back to her game of grains and tambourine, and like so many times that evening, counted and paired the grains over and over. After a considerable amount of time, when it seemed she could not find a way out of the grain maze, she picked up a handful of rice from the

bowl, poured them on a khata, mixed the grains from the tambourine, and again, as she was so prone to doing, spat profusely on the grains, tied them into a bundle and handed it over to the photographer. "Your mother's problem does not seem to be curable. The grains do not allow me to do so. I would suggest you to take her to the Tibetan doctors at Men Tsee Khang, but even that might not help. Here, take these

grains and make her have a pinchful of these with lukewarm water every morning and night. If she doesn't feel even slightly better off after a month, there is no point in consulting the doctors any further. I am sorry I am chained by the grains, if I don't obey their commands, I am afraid your mother's condition might worsen." A strange feeling engulfed the photographer when he heard these words translated by

the guide; he found himself swimming in a concoction of emotion mixed with dejection and relief, but above all he found himself happy.

Placing a hundred-rupee bill near Ayu Lhamo's feet, the photographer quietly got up from his seat on the floor, bowed before her and, silently waving at Burma, left the room.

The lane leading out of Ayu Lhamo's home was pitch dark by then. There were no street lights in the long winding path. Stumbling and half-guessing the way ahead only from the light that was spilling out of the windows by the lane, he headed towards the junction where the lane met the maddening market of Choglamsar. After a few minutes of walk, the path took a sharp right turn and he could see bright lights of the market ahead of him. It must have taken him hardly ten minutes of walk to reach where he was when he heard someone yelling at him from the darkness behind. It was Burma's guide with Burma in tow.

"Sir Burma tell me to call you. We drop you our vehicle to Leh. You
don't have vehicle, are you Sir!"

Burma just nodded at the photographer with a sad smile. The
photographer could not quite understand how in the world Ayu Lhamo
could dispense with Burma so soon. She surely did not give him even a
minute. Since it would be impolite to ask Burma about what transpired

within, the photographer did not mention anything on the way back. Burma too, for his part remained unusually quiet. Uneasy silence in human company has a certain way of affecting people. While the guide seated in the front row of the vehicle quietly hummed an unknown tune, the photographer found the silence in the vehicle asphyxiating, and was shuffling and shifting on the seat trying to think of something to

break the lull when suddenly Burma said, "you know what, this ol' lady of yours can see through everything, I'm tellin ya. Bet my past penny she can see what you had for dinner in your guts." The photographer burst out into a squawky laughter, throwing back his head. "No, really mate, how could she know about Michelle. Well she didn't get the name alright, but you know, what she said is spot on-just like that… bingo," Burma raised his fingers to form an imaginary pistol, and chattering away with his Australian drawl gave a brief handout of what happened after the photographer had left.

Ayu Lhamo did not even listen to Burma. She dismissed him at first sight. No amount of implorations from the guide could shake her resolve. She told the guide to tell his client that the Devil's sword shall fall on him if he even as much as utters a single word more. Angrily

waving, she told him he should not have left his partner in a country far far away when she was carrying his baby. She told him to return forthwith and seek her forgiveness, only then could he be healed. Ayu Lhamo called Burma names, and slammed expletives at him, all of which roughly translates to a selfish coward. The guide had dutifully translated every word of it to Burma.

As the vehicle trundled along, navigating the prime-time streets of Choglamsar, the rock-strewn debris around and the newly constructed flyover stood out like a grim reminder. That fateful night a few years back, when fifteen minutes of cloudburst had all but gobbled up Choglamsar, the monstrous mudslide carrying boulders the size of a sixteen-wheeler swept past Ayu Lhamo's neighbourhood without even hurting a twig.

May be she saw, may be the old lady sure does know.